Michael J. Fox

Colleen Hord

rourkeeducationalmedia.com

Teacher Notes available at
rem4teachers.com

www.rourkeeducationalmedia.com

PHOTO CREDITS: Cover, pages 4 - 8, 10 -12, 14 - 17, 19, 20: © AP Images; title page: © Laurence Agron; page 7: © Perkus; page 9: © Getty Images; page 13: © Wikipedia; page 18: © Darren Baker; page 19: © Lightwise; page 22: © Drserg

Edited by: Precious McKenzie

Cover and interior design by: Renee Brady

Library of Congress PCN Data

Michael J. Fox / Colleen Hord (Little World Biographies)
ISBN 978-1-61810-154-9 (hard cover)(alk. paper)
ISBN 978-1-61810-287-4 (soft cover)
ISBN 978-1-61810-411-3 (e-Book)
Library of Congress Control Number: 2011945880

Rourke Educational Media
Printed in the United States of America,
North Mankato, Minnesota

rourkeeducationalmedia.com

customerservice@rourkeeducationalmedia.com • PO Box 643328 Vero Beach, Florida 32964

Table of Contents

Optimism

Optimism is a favorite word of actor Michael J. Fox.

Optimism is the belief that even when you have problems, things will turn out for the best.

When Michael was young, he developed an optimistic attitude.

He had a dream to play professional hockey but everyone said he was too short to be a professional player.

Instead of being upset, he decided to join the drama club.

Michael J. Fox landed a job on the TV show Family Ties.

Michael's drama teacher thought he had acting talent and told him to try out for a TV series.

Michael J. Fox and Betty White at the Emmy Awards, 1986.

This started Michael's acting career. He won many acting awards and became very famous.

Michael won a Golden Globe award for Best Actor for his role in Spin City in 1999.

Parkinson's Disease

One morning, at the age of twenty-nine, Michael woke up and found that his pinky finger would not stop shaking.

Jean-Martin Charcot was a French neurologist. Charcot's studies between 1868 and 1881 is the earliest known research of Parkinson's disease.

His doctor told him he had an **incurable** disease called **Parkinson's**.

Still from *Secret of My Success.* 1994.

Even though his body would often shake, he continued to make movies and TV shows. He never gave up.

50th Annual Primetime Emmy Awards at the Shrine Auditorium in Los Angeles, Sunday, Sept. 13, 1998.

In 1998, Michael decided he would only act part time.

He wanted to spend more time with his family, and to find a cure for Parkinson's disease.

Michael J. Fox Foundation

TV Personality Stephen Colbert speaks at a benefit for the Michael J. Fox Foundation.

He started the Michael J. Fox **Foundation** for Parkinson's **Research**.

The foundation raises money so scientists
and doctors can find a cure for Parkinson's.

Books and Documentaries

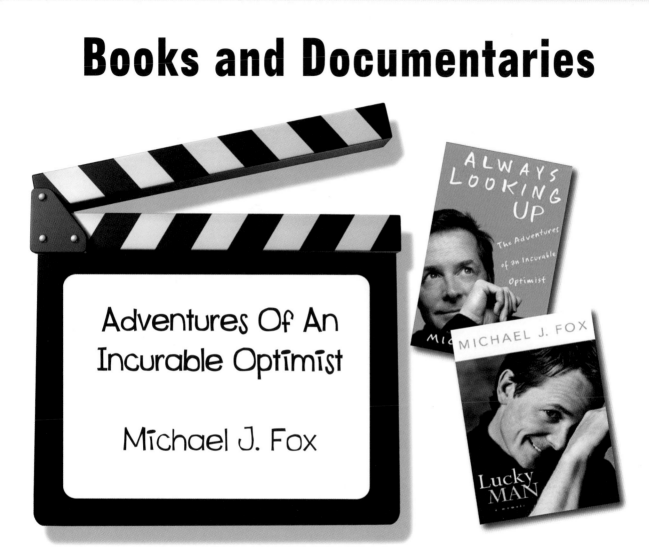

Adventures Of An
Incurable Optimist

Michael J. Fox

Michael also began writing books and
TV **documentaries**.

Michael wants to teach people to have hope and not give up when things go wrong.

Michael says he can't control his disease but he can control his attitude.

Timeline

1961	Michael born (June 9)
1982-89	Starred in TV show Family Ties
1988	Married Tracy Pollen
1991	Diagnosed with Parkinson's
1995	Received his GED
2000	Started the The Michael J. Fox Foundation for Parkinson's Research
2010	Won Grammy Award

Michael J. Fox encourages everyone to live each day with optimism.

Glossary

documentaries (dok-yuh-MEN-tuh-rees): movies or television programs made about real people

foundation (foun-DAY-shun): an organization that gives money to worthwhile causes

incurable (in-KYUR-uh-buhl): if someone has an incurable disease, the person cannot be made well

optimism (op-tuh-MISS-uhm): a belief that even when you have problems, things will work out for the best

Parkinson's (Par-kin-suhnz): an incurable disease causing tremors and involuntary movements

research (REE-surch): to study or find out about something

Index

Websites

www.michaeljfox.org

www.kidsinfo.com

www.scholastic.com

About the Author

Colleen Hord is an elementary teacher. Her favorite part of her teaching day is Writer's Workshop. She enjoys kayaking, camping, walking on the beach, and reading in her hammock.

Ask The Author!
www.rem4students.com